THE MALE TEENAGER'S 9 EARLY SIGNS OF ALCOHOLISM

*Becki Bateman,
with Dave Payne*

ALERT
(ACTUAL LEANING EXAMPLES TO RECOGNIZE TROUBLE) SERIES

Inspiring Voices®
A Service of **Guideposts**

Inspiring Voices books may be ordered through booksellers or by contacting:

Inspiring Voices
1663 Liberty Drive
Bloomington, IN 47403
www.inspiringvoices.com
1-(866) 697-5313

ISBN: 978-1-4624-0420-9 (sc)
ISBN: 978-1-4624-0419-3 (e)

Library of Congress Control Number: 2012921859

Printed in the United States of America

Inspiring Voices rev. date: 06/24/2013

L ife is a journey, not a destination. On my own marvelous journey, I have encountered so many people who have been the source of my inspiration, determination, and motivation. It would be impossible to name everyone responsible for helping me bring this dream to fruition. To Angie, Jenny, Carolyn, Mary Ellen, Mary, Peggy, Charlie, Ann, Melinda, and Melissa, my deepest gratitude!

I am most appreciative of the long-lasting love and friendship of L. M., who's been my personal muse for many years.

With deep pain (no pun intended, Dave) and heartfelt gratitude, this book is dedicated to Dave Payne, for his contribution to making this book a reality, for giving me the motivation to move the project "off the back burner and get cooking again," for his ability to balance the seriousness of a sobering subject with his wit and wisdom, and for providing the male perspective that was so invaluable for *The Male Teenager's 9 Early Signs of Alcoholism.* Certainly his scenarios were often more insightful from his viewpoint than mine.

Ironically, Dave was in hand-to-hand combat with his own disease the entire time we worked on this project. Unfortunately, he passed away as the book was moving into editorial review. Dave wanted to leave a lasting legacy. Hopefully his input into this series will be his greatest contribution, making a difference in a world that still doesn't understand how baffling, cunning, powerful, and insidious this disease truly is. He believed that young people need to recognize these early signs and become familiar with the available resources in order to get help earlier for this misunderstood malady.

Dave, thank you for your help. Your suggestions will continue to guide me and motivate me to complete the series in your memory.

ALSO BY THIS AUTHOR

ALERT (Actual Learning Examples to Recognize Trouble) Series:

> *The Male Teenager's 9 Early Signs of Alcoholism*
> *The Male Teenager's 9 Middle Signs of Alcoholism*
> *The Male Teenager's 9 Late Signs of Alcoholism*

Future publications:

The Female Teenager 9 Early Signs of Alcoholism
Female Teenager's Nine Middle Signs of Alcoholism
Female Teenager's Nine Late Signs of Alcoholism

H.I.N.T.S. (<u>H</u>elpful <u>I</u>nformation <u>N</u>eeded <u>T</u>o <u>S</u>ucceed) Series

Congratulations! You have picked out one of several titles in the ALERT (Actual Learning Examples to Recognize Trouble) series. After reading this first one, *Male Teenager's 9 Early Signs of Alcoholism,* you should have a better idea of how to recognize these early signals in a young man's behavior. Let's begin with some background information.

As you are reading, keep in mind that this series is not intended to be a collection of statistics or a rendering of research. With 232,000,000 sites on the Internet alone and thousands of books at local libraries and bookshops, we suggest you gather information as it relates to and interests you. At the end of each book in the series, there are listed resources and Web sites where you can gather pertinent information relevant to your personal journey.

In the 80s, when the subject of alcoholism became popular on TV talk shows, in the movies, and in books on alcoholism, codependency, and adult children of alcoholics, there a huge explosion of knowledge; many of the books made it to the best-seller lists. At the same time, national conferences such as the Annual Conference on Alcoholism and the Family as well as Adult Children of Alcoholics drew focus to this problem. Unfortunately, over the next thirty years the hoopla died down, but the problem has not. A vast amount of people still carry a stereotype of what a "typical" alcoholic looks and acts like.

If you are asked to close your eyes and picture an alcoholic, do you picture an old person on a street corner begging for money, a homeless person sleeping under a bridge or a piece of cardboard, or someone eating out of a dumpster? When you picture alcoholics, are they all male? Such images would not be entirely wrong; however, you would be picturing alcoholics in chronic or late-stage alcoholism, which is only 3 percent of the alcoholic population. No one wakes up in the chronic stage of alcoholism; each and every drinker has had to go through the early and middle stages first.

Statistically, it's roughly 50 percent male and 50 percent female today who are an alcoholic. Younger and younger people are being treated for this affliction. Alcoholism doesn't discriminate. It'll take any age, color, ethnic group, or occupation into its grip. For example, did you envision any professionals such as a doctor, nurse, teacher, lawyer, or clergyman? Name any occupation, and 10 percent are alcoholics in one of the three stages. They are referred to as functioning alcoholics.

Functioning alcoholics are people who do not show any clear signs of having a problem. They perform well while on the job, are rarely absent, and often are cited for exemplary work. Some specific examples of those working in the helping professions and in one of three stages of alcoholism are:

- a teacher who comes to work every day and is a "weekend warrior", that is, drinks heavily on weekends

- a lawyer whose caseload is 79 percent alcohol related and works to help alcoholics and yet he nips throughout the day
- a counselor who helps scores of young men and women with their problems dealing with alcohol and has alcohol hidden in drawers and on shelves at work
- a nurse who tends sick alcoholics on a daily basis and immediately begins drinking as soon as she goes home
- a doctor who diagnoses and treats patients for the disease while hiding his own alcoholism.

The list could go on and on, as 10 percent of people in any given occupation are alcoholic. Family, friends, and clients have absolutely no idea of the functioning alcoholic's dependence on alcohol.

One of the most profound quotes comes from Father Joseph Martin, who is well-known in the field of alcoholism. He stated, "By the time an alcoholic is in chronic-stage alcoholism, any moron would know he's got a problem; that's only 3 percent of the alcoholic population. We, as a society, need to be more informed about the other 97 percent that aren't in chronic alcoholism but have the potential to be."

Many people in the 97 percent could be teenagers, yet this age group has not been adequately addressed. Teens in general have a tougher time identifying with alcoholism. They can give many reasons why they're *not* alcoholics. They're too young; they haven't experienced loss of things such as jobs, families, or homes; they haven't gotten kicked out of school or been in jail or prison. They only party on the weekends like everyone else does, or they "only have a couple" once in awhile. Teens don't recognize the early signs of alcoholism.

If teens don't have a job to lose, haven't started their own families, and haven't acquired an abundance of material things they won't have losses that can indicate earlier problems one can experience with drinking. A great number if teens aren't likely to do anything illegal or create enough problems to warrant getting arrested. If they do run into legal issues, they rely on their parents. Yet Mom and Dad will often deny that their kids have a problem. They may defend their son or daughter or bail him or her out of jail so their child doesn't suffer any consequences for his or her behavior.

There are signs that have been indentified to help recognize alcoholism, nine signs in each of the three stages (early, middle, and late) for a total of twenty seven. How many teens would know any of them? More importantly, would they be able to cite specific examples in their own drinking patterns related to these signs?

In reality, each person is different, so the examples presented in this book could not possibly demonstrate all the ways a young person shows early symptoms of this disease.

Each of the nine signs will be presented with three or more possible scenarios in which a teenage young man named J. D. exhibits the symptoms in these early stages. As you read this, try to identify with each scenario instead of comparing. In other words, look for ways you are like the teen in the example, not ways you are different. If you are reading this because you are concerned about a friend or relative who may be experiencing problems with alcohol, try to think of this person, how he or she would exhibit each one of the early signs, and how you might be of help.

Keep in mind that every teen will progress at a different rate. He could remain in the early stage for ten to twenty years or for as little as a year or even less, depending upon many variables (e.g., the age he began drinking, his body chemistry, his height and weight, the amount he drinks, how often he drinks, what he drinks, what, if any, other substances he ingests while drinking, etc.).

Another ten to twenty years can be spent in the next phase of the disease. The final stage can span the same amount of time. That is, if a teen started drinking at age thirteen, he could be in the early stage until thirty-three; middle stage would see him go from age thirty-three to fifty-three; and the last stage would take him into his sixties and beyond. This explains why one usually thinks of an alcoholic as someone old.

It is not unusual for a teen to begin drinking before the age of thirteen. The younger a person is when he picks up the drink, the faster it affects him; his body, bones, and organs are still forming. A teen who weighs 95 pounds will progress through the stages faster than a young person weighing 140 pounds or more. The five-foot-two-inch teen will also progress faster than the teen who is six feet tall. A young person who drinks daily will show signs more quickly than a teen who drinks a couple of bottles of wine three or four times a week. If other substances (drugs or pills, for example) are used while the young man is drinking, he will rapidly progress. Considering such factors, it is possible to go through the early stages of alcoholism in five years or less—if he begins using at thirteen he might enter the middle stage around eighteen, and he could be in the late stages of addiction by the early age of twenty-three! Again, each person's inner chemical makeup reacts differently to the alcohol and the substances that he takes into his body.

Here's a quick overview of each stage and its symptoms:

The nine early signs:

1. Hide it
2. Sneak it/steal it
3. Angry when someone tries to talk about the drinking
4. Blame other people, places, and things
5. Drink when something bad/good happens
6. Drink until supply is gone
7. Change in personality
8. Uncomfortable when not available
9. Blackouts

The nine middle signs:

1. Drink before a function
2. Lose interest in other things
3. Preoccupation with drinking
4. Fail repeatedly to keep promises and resolutions
5. Neglect personal care (hygiene/food/health)
6. Problems with family, friends, work, school, and money
7. Increased tolerance
8. Increased dependence
9. Blackouts—more frequent, longer in duration

The nine late signs:

1. Loss of family, friends, and jobs
2. Loss of willpower and control
3. Obsession with use
4. Physical and moral deterioration
5. Decreased intolerance
6. Drinking with people he considers beneath him or alone
7. Impaired thinking
8. Geographical cures
9. Mental health facilities, hospitals, jails, or death

So now let's meet J. D., a typical thirteen-year-old-teenager. He is the middle child; he has a brother who is three years older than him and a sister who is a couple years younger. His brother, A. J., has a wide range of interests, and friends seem to flock to him. It helps that he is class president and excels in sports. A. J. always gets good grades effortlessly, so he doesn't spend much time studying. J. D.'s sister, D. D., drives him crazy with her preteen hormones. She looks up to both her brothers and tries to tag along with them any chance she gets. His dad is a lab technician, and his mom is a social worker. They look like the typical all-American family, but J. D. never felt he measured up to his big brother. He never felt like he fit in.

His parents have never talked to him about drinking, but he knew his mother hated alcohol because her dad had been a mean drunk who died of alcoholism. His paternal grandmother had been an at-home drinker, and his dad didn't feel comfortable inviting his friends to his house because he never knew what she'd be like. But J. D. never realized that there were alcohol problems on both sides of his family.

He had grown up in a home where there was a "don't ask, don't tell, and don't feel" code within the family. He was expected not to ask any questions, especially regarding what happened when someone in his house drank too much. He couldn't talk about what was really bothering him to anyone outside the family—this was seen as airing the family's dirty laundry. And he was not allowed to feel. He was constantly told, "You'll be given something to cry about," "Real men don't cry," and "Don't be a sissy." So he was taught to ignore his emotions and would shut down.

He doesn't have a clue that he may be more prone to the disease of alcoholism growing up in an alcoholic family; he has a 50 percent chance of becoming an alcoholic, marrying one, or both.

J. D.'s first drink was a result of a challenge from one of his friends when he was thirteen. Not wanting his pal to question his manhood or call him a wimp, J. D. drank that first one right down. He will always remember how it tasted, but the tingling sensation right down to his toes is the most memorable part of the experience. He chugged more until he staggered to the bathroom and threw up. He vowed he'd never drink like that again. Suddenly J. D. was no longer a misfit. The more he drank, the more acceptable he became; in his mind, he was now the smartest, the funniest, and the best-looking of all his friends. Now let's see how J. D.'s drinking demonstrates every one of the early signs of alcoholism.

1. HIDE IT

The first sign of early alcoholism is hiding the alcohol. J. D. hides his alcohol in a soda bottle or any other container to make it look like he's drinking something other than booze. Vodka could very easily be added to a bottle of soda, and no one would be the wiser. J. D. believes he is very clever when he dumps out a can of cola and replaces the liquid inside with beer. This makes it very easy for him to hide his alcohol in his hall or gym locker at school. He could drink right in front of people, and they wouldn't have a clue!

He could also hide his stash in various secret spots throughout the house, so it would be easily accessible when he needed to take a drink. It might be hidden in a rarely used cupboard in the pantry. He could even put some cans on a high shelf in the corner of his bedroom, cover them, and place other objects in front of them. Some alcohol could be hidden behind the taller books on his desk or in the back of his closet, covered with clothes, where no one would ever suspect. Since it is seldom used, the cellar is another ideal spot for J. D. to keep his extra supply.

J. D. is smart enough to know he needs hiding spots both inside and outside the house. Behind his home, there is a shed that is rarely used, and he has access to the key. There are some boxes in which he can hide bottles or cans. All he has to do is bury them in the bottom of the box and replace the items back on top. On one of the top shelves in this shed is a box marked "Scrapbooks." He hides some bottles of liquor at the very bottom and covers them with a couple books of memorabilia. Another clever hiding spot was a cooler in the corner. If this stash was ever discovered, he could deny he knew anything about it and say that it must have been left there from another time the family had used it. The garage is filled with terrific hiding spots. Empty storage cabinets, crates, cardboard boxes, totes, storage bins, and empty toolboxes provide J. D. with plenty of ways to disguise his supply of alcohol. He's confident he will not have to worry about anyone discovering any of these hiding places.

Suppose someone walks into a room where J. D. is drinking, and he immediately stashes his drink behind a chair or a curtain. That's another signal. Would he have to hide a glass of soda, milk, or juice? Perhaps he gets someone else to buy his alcohol, as he is not of legal age. It is even more apparent he is beginning to exhibit some of the early signs of alcoholism if he gets three or four different people of legal age to secretly keep him with an adequate supply of beer, wine, or liquor. Whether he is hiding the alcohol itself, drinking in secret, or having others buy his liquor, J. D. is concealing his use.

Now, can you come up with more ways teenage boys hide their use?

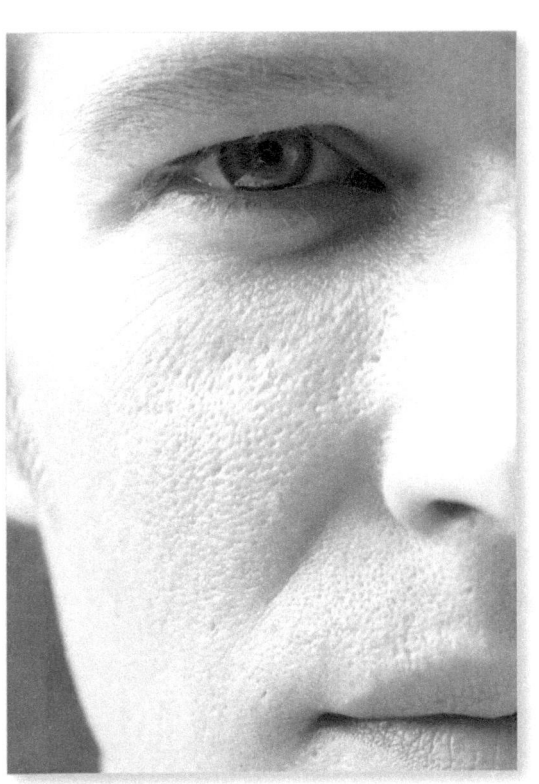

2. SNEAK IT/STEAL IT

J. D. knows where the key to his parents' liquor cabinet is, and will sneak some of the hard stuff once in a while. When he takes the alcohol out of any bottle, he always remembers to water it down so his parents won't notice anything missing. He is careful not to do this too often, so his parents are less likely to catch on.

He doesn't dare bring a case of beer into the house. He is afraid someone might catch him, so he sneaks in a six pack at a time or hides just a couple of cans in his jacket.

It is also handy that one of his uncles has a bar in his basement. He will make an excuse to go down and sneak a couple swigs. Sometimes he'll go down with an empty bottle, pour some liquor into it, and take it home. Then he'll pour it into a bigger container; this way he'd eventually have enough to get drunk by himself or take this supply to a party.

Eventually, J. D. starts to steal from his relatives. First he takes money out of his mother's wallet. He also knows where his grandparents hide some cash, and once in a while, he will "borrow" it to buy booze. He has every intention of paying them back.

On one occasion, J. D. and his friends decided to break into a house. There were many items they could have stolen, but they only took beer and liquor.

One of his drinking buddies works at a convenience store. While the friend is working his shift, J. D. waits until his friend has another customer and hides a bottle of wine under his jacket. Then he hollers good-bye to his buddy and walks off with the booze as his friend looks the other way. After his shift is over, his friend stops by J. D.'s, and they share the stolen bottle. J. D. has even stolen some of his friends' beer when he knew he could get away with it. Obviously the booze is more important than his friendships. When J. D. steals the alcohol, he doesn't give a thought to the consequences—his actions might be endangering his friend's job, risking his friendships, or getting him into trouble.

What other examples can you think of a teen sneaking or stealing alcohol or cash to use to purchase alcohol that would indicate a potential problem?

3. Angry When Someone Tries To Talk About The Drinking

J. D. began dating a girl when he was fifteen. She thought there were times he drank too much and tried to talk to him about it. He broke up with her because he considered her a drag and a nag. A good friend, who was also concerned about J. D.'s behavior when he was drinking, tried to discuss it with him. When the subject is brought up, J. D. gets very angry and defensive. He hollers, screams, calls his friend names, and refuses to listen to reason. J. D. begins hanging out with him less and less, spending more time with people who are more accepting of his lifestyle.

J. D.'s parents notice a definite change in the type of friends that he's hanging out with in his free time. They are concerned that he is withdrawing and isolating himself; they notice a change in his attitude and a drop in his grades. They try to talk to him about it, but J. D. only gets angry and more disrespectful of them. They try to reason with him, and that only pushes him further away.

A teacher questions J. D.'s grades, which have been dropping in his class. J. D. had started out the first half of the year on the honor roll. His grades plunged to mid-Cs, and he scored even lower on a couple of tests. Another teacher brings up his poor attendance; he is missing at least one day a week, and it's usually on a Friday. Yet another of his teachers is concerned because of his behavior. When the teachers try to talk to him about these concerns, he has a fit and says that his teachers just don't understand him and are singling him out. Finally he is called into the counselor's office. When that doesn't seem to do any good, the principal tries discussing everyone's concerns about this change in J. D.'s entire attitude.

A club advisor notices J. D. isn't attending the weekly meetings and questions his reasons, but J. D. offers only a few lame excuses, so he is asked to resign. J. D. doesn't tell the advisor that he is leaving school early to be with kids who have a reputation for partying after school.

What other examples can you think of for this early warning sign?

4. BLAME OTHER PEOPLE, PLACES, AND THINGS

J. D. gets into trouble because of his drinking episodes and is quick to point the finger at other people, places, and things. He immediately tries to blame it on someone else. On one occasion, he was at a party, drank too much, and blamed it on his friends, saying they must have spiked his drink because he hadn't had enough to get so loaded. Another time, after a basketball game, he blamed his buddies for him not getting in on time. His curfew was eleven o'clock, and he ran into his house at twelve forty-five saying he'd had to wait for his friends for a ride home. In reality, they'd found him highly intoxicated, and he gave them a really hard time about leaving. They had tried to sober him up, but when his parents questioned the condition J. D. was in, he blamed everything on his friends.

A. J. also notices changes in his younger brother. He tries numerous times to talk to him about his lack of interest in doing anything with the family; J. D. says they never ask him to go anywhere either. When A. J. mentions J. D.'s habit of staying out of the house more and more, J. D. blames this on no one being home anyway.

J. D. got his first part-time job at a neighborhood grocery store when he was fifteen. To earn extra money, he could work limited hours stacking shelves. After he was fired, he immediately went out, got drunk, and blamed the boss He wouldn't admit that he lost the job because he kept making excuses for not showing up to work or being late due to drinking.

J. D. got his second part-time job at a fast-food chain as soon as he turned sixteen. He wanted to earn extra money because he planned to get his driver's license, buy a used car, and have money for gas and insurance. After school, he'd throw down a couple drinks to get "ready" to go to work. He would shortly begin to mess up the orders. As his buzz wore off, he'd become more agitated with the customers, at which time his boss would confront him. After J. D. repeatedly showed up "ready" for work, he was again let go. Of course, he was in complete denial as to why he lost this job.

J. D. also likes to cite school as a reason to drink. He blames teachers for being too strict, his classes for being extremely boring, other kids for making fun of him, and hundreds of other things in the school setting that he believes drive him to drink.

Outside of school, he often gets frustrated when his computer fails to work properly. He relieves this stress by going into his closet and getting an immediate fix from his stash. He also feels very self-conscious about his newest problem, acne. He thinks everyone is talking behind his back about his pimples. When he drinks the pimples "fall off" and he's convinced that this is the only way to overcome his discomfort; all he has to do is take a couple drinks before going to school to gain some courage to deal with what he thinks everyone is whispering about behind his back.

Can you come up with a few examples of blaming people, places, or something else for your drinking?

5. DRINK WHEN SOMETHING BAD/GOOD HAPPENS

It was extremely sad when J. D.'s grandfather passed away. J. D. had spent a lot of time with him growing up because his grandparents lived right around the corner from his house. His grandfather had been diagnosed with cancer when J. D. was twelve. He had watched the disease physically, emotionally, and mentally destroy his grandfather in those final years. After his grandfather passed away from the painful disease, J. D. left the funeral parlor and escaped to a secluded spot and proceeded to get good and drunk. He was too hung over to attend the funeral. Then, less than a month later, a good childhood friend was killed in a car accident. The only way he knew how to ease the pain was to escape into a bottle.

J. D. was extremely disappointed when he was unexpectedly cut from his football team. To deal with his anger, he went to the city park and began yelling obscenities at the senior citizens who lived in the high rise next to the park. He smashed beer bottles as soon as he drank them. Finally he was arrested for disorderly conduct and taken into custody. His parents were notified, and they refused to bail him out, thinking that this would teach him a lesson. However, it only made J. D. angrier.

When J. D. failed an important test, he called up a few friends and invited them to party, suggesting he'd supply the booze.

These are a few examples of when a teen might drink when something bad happens. Can you think of some more to add to these?

On the flip side, J. D. is looking forward to June 9. School would be getting out for the summer, and he and his friends have been planning a big bonfire and a keg for the occasion. They are going to celebrate, and they have all put aside money, not only for the keg, but for quite an assortment of other alcoholic beverages. This would really kick off the summer season!

After taking a science test with a hangover, J. D. was sure he had failed it. He could hardly believe it when his name was read as having one of the five highest grades. He couldn't wait to get out of school to get into his private stash and celebrate.

J. D.'s team won the regional championship in baseball. He and his teammates are going to celebrate this in a big way. Everyone is going to meet at the captain's parents' cottage and bring something to drink. J. D. expects it will be a blast!

No one was more shocked than J. D. when he was given an award at the end-of-year school assembly. He could hardly contain his excitement to get together with his friends so they could all celebrate. This will be a great opportunity to get some really good stuff.

A teen can think of many excuses to drink when good things happens also. Can you add to the list?

6. DRINK UNTIL SUPPLY IS GONE

J. D. buys a couple six packs, and although he gets pretty wasted, he still drinks until the last can is gone. This is yet another symptom of early-stage alcoholism.

Another time J. D. was at a family wedding. He went around the tables where people had left, and he gulped down what was remaining in their glasses. He couldn't understand why anyone could leave any amount of good booze in a glass and walk away from it. This is another example of drinking until supply is gone.

Sometimes J. D. and his friends get together for a friendly poker game on Friday nights. Often the game ends up being played in his garage, and there's always some booze. After everyone leaves, J. D. drinks the leftovers; leftovers just mean more for him!

How many more examples can you name?

7. CHANGE IN PERSONALITY

Another early warning sign is if there is a definite change in a teen's personality when he drinks.

J. D. loves the feeling that drinking gives him; he can be anyone he wants to be. As the middle child, he feels like A. J. and D. D. get all the attention. He's a good student, but tons of other kids get recognized and rewarded for their good grades. He never feels like he fits in anywhere, but once he takes that first drink, he feels accepted and confident. When he walks into a room of strangers, it doesn't take him long to figure out how to act around them.

By nature J. D. is shy, but once he's had a couple drinks his attitude changes and he becomes very defensive. His beer muscles take over, and he challenges anyone larger than himself to step outside. Soon J. D. begins to not only pick fights with strangers, but starts turning on his friends.

When J. D. first began drinking, he always enjoyed the company of his buddies. As time went on he began to drink more and with more frequency than his friends. He was drinking alone, telling himself that there was more for him to drink; he doesn't need anything but his booze and his music.

J. D. drinks when he's irritated, angry, unhappy, or frustrated so the alcohol will kill all those feelings. Out of the blue, he reacts in anger when someone says something that wouldn't bother anyone else, but even he doesn't understand what's happening to him.

Do these changes in J. D.'s behavior when drinking affect those around him? What other kinds of changes are noticeable when he drinks?

8. Uncomfortable When Not Available

J. D. exhibits another early warning sign of alcoholism when he chooses not to go to places where alcohol won't be available. He doesn't think he could possibly have a good time at any school function if he isn't able to drink, so he brings a flask along in case he needs some liquid courage. Although all family functions—weddings, funerals, picnics, family reunions, and even kids' birthday parties—seem to include alcohol, J. D. takes his flask to these gatherings as well, because he's making sure that he'll have his own supply and not have to worry how he'll get it when needed.

He doesn't go to certain friends' houses when invited because he knows their parents don't approve of underage drinking. As a result, he is drifting away from the guys he's been pals with since elementary school and hanging out more with guys who are older and like to party.

J. D. can't imagine going to any party where there isn't going to be drinking—how else would he be able to talk or ask any girl to dance?

Can you name some specific situations in which a teenage boy thinks he needs a couple drinks to fit in?

9. Blackouts

Not all drinkers experience this last early warning sign of alcoholism, but it can be a major indicator. It's called a blackout; this means a person can function but will not remember what he's done or might only recall parts of it when he sobers up.

For example, J. D. went to a party knowing he had a curfew, but he drank too much and lost track of time. He checked his watch, realized he had to get home, and ran through every shortcut to get there. When he entered the house, he hollered to his parents that he was home and stumbled upstairs to bed. However, when he woke the next morning, he had no recollection of how he got home and remembered only bits and pieces of what happened at the party.

Another time, J. D. woke up on the floor at his friend's house; he had absolutely no idea how he had ended up there. He'd remembered he and his friend had gone to a party. There were plenty of available girls and he intended to ask this real cute chick for a dance. The last thing he remembered was the trip to the backyard to take a nip from his flask to get the courage to ask her.

On one occasion, J. D. was involved in a minor accident while driving someone else's car. Not only did he not have his license or even a permit, but he couldn't remember why he was driving in the first place. One of his buddies had asked him to drive because his friend was way too drunk. J. D. couldn't recall anything when the police questioned him on the scene. He was taken to the police station and called several friends to help him. However, after several refusals from his buddies he resorted to calling his parents to bail him out of jail.

One morning he awoke fully clothed in his bed, and his clothes were covered with dirt and leaves. When he went into the bathroom and peered into the mirror, he saw that he had bumps and bruises on his face and all over his body. Where did they come from? He didn't have a clue. He thought that he might find out what happened if he called one of his buddies.

Most teens confuse blacking out with passing out. Passing out means just that—a person drinks to the point where he becomes unconscious, and it may be on his bed, the living room floor, or a neighbor's lawn. However, a blackout is when activity continues even though the memories aren't retained. In other words, the person appears to be functioning normally, but when the teen tries to recall people, places, things, and actions from while he was drunk, he is unable to do so reliably. When he checks with his friends to find out what happened, they assure him he was the life of the party.

Can you think of some other examples that indicate this last warning sign?

Many young people fail to recognize these early signs of alcoholism, but once you are aware of what to look for, you can see a potential problem and get help early. If you recognize two or more of these symptoms in one of your friends or even yourself as you read about J. D., ask for help. Remember, alcoholism is the only disease known to man that the longer you have this addiction, the more it convinces you that you don't!

Now that you are more aware of the early signs of alcoholism, you may want to check out the next book in this series, *The Male Teenager's 9 Middle Signs of Alcoholism.*

Father Joseph Martin said, "If you had a friend or relative with cancer or other serious disease, wouldn't you get your hands on everything you could to help them? I suggest you do the same thing with the disease of alcoholism." With that quote in mind, here a few resources you can go to for further information:

Check the Yellow Pages for *Alcoholics Anonymous, alcoholism, treatment centers, Reach Out, rehabilitation services,* or, in the government offices section, found in front of phone book, see the listing under "county" for *alcohol/substance abuse services* or *chemical dependency services* or the listing under "state" for the health care hotline. Your local hospitals can also provide more information.

If you have never attended a meeting or group, try to go to at least a dozen different meetings at first, to get a feel for which one you can relate to the best. Unfortunately, many people have preconceived notions about these groups that are not always true. Go to a meeting telling yourself you will learn at least one thing; if you identify with anyone or with any topic discussed, consider attending that group again; if you think you didn't learn anything, try going to another meeting in your area. Try not to convince yourself that some of the suggestions won't work for you before you try any. There are over a hundred self-help groups that can further your understanding. The following are some of the most widely known for alcoholism:

Alanon— The only requirement for membership is that there is a problem with alcoholism in a relative or friend.

Alateen— The only requirement for membership is that there be a problem with alcoholism in a relative or friend.

Alcoholics Anonymous— The only requirement for membership is a desire to stop drinking.

Children of Alcoholics or Adult Children of Alcoholics— A program of men and women who grew up in an alcoholic or other dysfunctional homes.

Co-Dependents Anonymous – The only requirement for membership is a desire for healthy and loving relationships.

Families Anonymous—A program of families and friends who have known a feeling of desperation concerning the destructive behavior of someone very near to them whether caused by drugs, alcohol, or other related behaviors.

Some prominent people have made significant contributions in the field of alcoholism and addiction. An Internet search and a review of their Wikipedia pages will help you find valuable information. The following eight people are now deceased, but have left a lasting legacy in the field:

Betty Ford—the outspoken First Lady who founded Betty Ford Treatment Center

Ernie Larsen—best known for his Stage II Recovery process

Marty Mann—the "First Lady of Alcoholics Anonymous," who went on to found the National Council on Alcoholism

Father Joseph Martin—a Roman Catholic priest, recovered alcoholic, and renowned speaker known for his video, *Chalk Talk on Alcohol*

M. Scott Peck—the author of *The Road Less Traveled* and fourteen other books

Dr. Robert Smith— cofounder of Alcoholics Anonymous

Bill Wilson—cofounder of Alcoholics Anonymous

Janet Woititz—know for her extensive work concerning adult children of alcoholics

The following people are among the many still active in the field, writing, teaching, training, speaking, or conducting workshops and seminars:

Melody Beattie—best known for her book *Codependent No More: How to Stop Controlling Others and Start Caring for Yourself* (www.melodybeattie.com)

Claudia Black—best known for her book *"It Will Never Happen to Me" Children of Alcoholics: As Youngsters—Adolescents—Adults* (www.claudiablack.com)

John Bradshaw—hosted numerous programs on PBS based on his books (www.johnbradshaw.com)

Sharon Wegscheider-Cruse—best known for her book *Another Chance: Hope and Health for the Alcoholic Family* (www.sharonwcruse.com)

John Lee—best known for his book *The Flying Boy: Healing the Wounded Man* (www.johnleebooks.com)

Robert Subby—best known for his book *Lost in the Shuffle*

If you do an Internet search for "films about alcohol and alcoholism," you will be given the names of some classic ones, such as *The Lost Weekend*, *Days of Wine and Roses,* and *Leaving Las Vegas*. Other films worth looking into include *My Name is Bill W.,* the story of Alcoholics Anonymous cofounder Bill Wilson, and *When Love Is Not Enough,* the story of Lois Wilson, founder of Alanon and wife of Bill Wilson.

There are over 232,000,000 Web sites that result from a search just on "statistics for alcoholism," so you can see why it would be impossible to list them all. Here are some search terms to get you started:

Alcohol abuse
Current statistics on alcoholism
Adult alcohol abuse

Alcoholism
National statistics on alcoholism
Alcohol statistics by race
Alcohol-related deaths
Alcoholism family statistics
Statistics on alcohol in America
Alcohol consumption
Alcohol parent statistics

Of course, libraries are an excellent resource, as they have books, cassettes, magazines, books on tape, CDs, and DVDs on alcohol and alcoholism.

It is our sincere hope that this list of resources will enhance your journey to sobriety.

About The Author

Becki Bateman earned a BS and an MA in education in the 60's and early 70's. It was at the beginning of 1978 that she began her own personal recovery journey. The only reason she went to a meeting for anyone having a friend or relative with a drinking problem was to find an answer to get those people causing chaos, calamities, and crisis in her life to straighten up so she'd be okay! While attending those meetings she got to see videos, read books, and hear material on the family disease of alcoholism. One quote from Father Joseph Martin in one of his videos was "Never be impressed with people who hold degrees; after all rectal thermometers have them and you know where they put them."

In the early 80s, after taking courses in an alcohol and chemical dependency studies program at a local college, she was introduced to the early, middle, and late signs of the disease of alcoholism. This was the first time with all her education she not only realized what a stereotype she had of an alcoholic, but also recognized how angry she was at the educational system because it had not taught her about the one subject that had affected her life more than anything else. Around this same time she also began driving clients from a local rehab to another twelve-step program, where she heard others' stories. At first she compared herself to them, but slowly she started to identify when she'd heard them talk of some of their own experiences.

She was a slow learner; after four and a half years of going meetings to learn how to help others with their problem with alcohol and another year in the other meetings strictly as a "volunteer" did she experience a wake-up call. Eventually Becki realized that she also belonged in the latter program.

Thus, her knowledge does not come from reading tons of books or paying thousands of dollars for classes; it comes primarily from being an active listener in a multitude of meetings in four different self-help programs, conferences, retreats, and workshops in a wide variety of places. She heard people share honestly of their pain, their denial, their experiences, their strength, and their hope. These experiences are the foundation of her journey that could have given her a PhD in the study of alcoholism. She became a student in the "University of Life". Some say that experience is the best teacher, but she has learned that experience is the only teacher.

Recognizing her own alcoholism was a major turning point in her life. Not only did it have a major impact on her personal life, but it enhanced her abilities as a teacher. She touched her student's lives in a way she never could have imagined. She could now recognize the "overachiever", "scapegoat", "lost child", and "mascot" in her classrooms. She incorporated some of her lessons around subject matter relating to alcohol or alcoholism. For example, she had them write about the four stages of alcoholism. Becki gained some of the children's trust so those who were living in a home with the three ground rules - don't ask, don't talk, and don't feel - could express themselves and reveal their feelings.

This journey has spanned over three decades, during which she attended numerous conferences and workshops. Some of the most significant were ACCEPT '81 (Atlantic City Conference on Education & Prevention Techniques). ACCEPT '83, and Annual Conferences on Alcoholism and the Family from 1982 through 1986. In 1986, the conference changed its name to the Annual Conference on Chemical Dependency and the Family because the coordinators realized it didn't matter the substance; the dynamics affecting the families living with any addiction were basically the same. In 1985, she went out to California and attended TRIBES, a program which taught people how to work cooperatively in groups. She was the only person east of the Ohio River to be qualified as a trainer of trainers. In 1986, she attended the National Youth to Youth Conference in Ohio and the Family Restoration Workshop with Sharon Wegscheider-Cruise. In 1987, she went to the Third Annual Conference for Adult Children of Alcoholics. She was selected as an adult staff member for the Annual Youth to Youth Conferences in 1987–1989, where she quickly became known as "the warm fuzzy lady," and in August 1988, she attended the First Annual Western Youth to Youth Conference in California. In November 1989, she attended the Codependency and Intimate Relationship Conference in Florida.

In the early '90s, Becki and another coworker planned a Superintendent's Day on alcohol awareness. She remains active and the following article adds a little more to her accomplishments and illustrates how helping others allows her to pass on what she has been so freely given.

VOLUNTEER

Reprint of 1999 article)
Taken from the Hamilton Hall Herald, a newsletter of St.
Lawrence Alcoholism Treatment Center
December Issue 5

Variety is the spice of life, says an old adage. Until recently I didn't realize the extent of volunteer work I had done throughout my life.

Once upon a time I began my volunteering in a nursing home during high school. It has continued to the present day in various ways. During the growing-up years of my two daughters, I taught Sunday school, eventually becoming Superintendent of Sunday Schools.

Late in the 1970s, I became a volunteer at the St. Lawrence Alcoholism Treatment Center. I drove patients to outside 12-step meetings, made a rotating schedule coordinating seven other volunteers, and got a dozen or more new recruits so more meetings were available to the clients at the rehab.

Understanding more and more about addiction from attending numerous national conferences, workshops, retreats, I began a community prevention program called AIM AHEAD (An Involvement of Many—Awareness and Helping in the Education of Alcohol and other Drugs). Another important accomplishment was writing a weekly column in the At Your Leisure section of the local Sunday paper. The articles were all related to addiction and ran about five years.

Next, I began to share this information using another format. I made presentations and did trainings. One presentation was Expanding Our Horizons in Prevention at the 1986 NYFAC (New York Federation of Alcoholism Counselors) Conference. I also trained the local treatment center staff on Communication and Listening Skills for STAFF (Strategies and Techniques Affecting a Facility's Fellowship).

Then I served on different committees and boards. St Lawrence County was the largest county in New York State and the only one without a council. Serving on the original committee to establish a council for alcoholism, I was elected in 1986 to be on the first Board of Directors of the Alcohol and Substance Abuse Council of St. Lawrence County and was honored to be its president for two years. In addition I was asked to serve on the board of the North Country Freedom Homes, the Advisory Committee to the Mater Dei College Alcohol and Chemical Dependency Program, and also on the Community Advisory Board at the local treatment center.

Energetic, eager, earnest, teens kept me young at heart from 1985–1996 while working with Youth to Youth and YES (Youth Educating Society). A weekend every month or so found me, aka The Warm Fuzzy Lady" at a Youth to Youth conference in a high school in and around my county in New York State. The highlight was going to Russia and Ireland with a group of 50 teens and staff for a couple weeks in 1992 and with another similar group to Australia in 1995.

Every Thursday night from 1992–1999, I taught a recovery workshop at the local treatment center. "I've found GOD" (Good Orderly Direction), "I am not NUTS" (Not Using the Steps), and "I use TOOLS" (Techniques Offering Options with Love and Support) were just a few of the topics shared. Another project undertaken at this local treatment center was to gather recovery materials for the facility's library.

Recognized with awards such as volunteer of the year at the treatment center for 1994 and 1995 was a great honor. Then in 1999 I was awarded the volunteer of the year for the Northern Tier Providers Association of Alcohol and Substance Abuse Services. (Given to an individual who has given of their time and talent to provide assistance to the client community, promote community treatment and/or prevention efforts or advocate on behalf of those in need.)

NOTES

NOTES

NOTES

NOTES